Photography
Colour Library Books
The Glenn Harvey Picture Collection

Design
Philip Clucas, MSIAD

Commissioning Editor
Andrew Preston

Commissioning
Laura Potts

Editorial
Gill Waugh
Fleur Robertson

Production
Ruth Arthur
David Proffit
Sally Connolly
Andrew Whitelaw

Director of Production
Gerald Hughes

CLB 2570
© 1991 Colour Library Books Ltd, Godalming, Surrey, England.
All rights reserved.
This 1991 edition published by Crescent Books,
distributed by Outlet Book Company, Inc, a Random House Company,
225 Park Avenue South, New York, New York 10003.
Color separations by Scantrans Pte Ltd, Singapore.
Printed and bound in Singapore.
ISBN 0 517 06607 6
8 7 6 5 4 3 2 1

THE ROYAL FAMILY

The royal coat of arms as it appears on
one of the ceremonial carriages used
by the Royal Family.

THE ROYAL FAMILY

JANE MASTERSON

CRESCENT BOOKS
NEW YORK

IT HAS BEEN CALLED a soap opera and a business, depending on the point of view of the commentator. But, however you look at the Royal Family, it is a unique institution which is set firmly in the hearts of the British people, and many overseas.

THE ROYAL FAMILY IS not just a collection of individuals, nor even a family group – it is an institution of state. The constitution of Britain depends upon the monarch and without her could not function. The position places enormous burdens of duty on this family which they fulfil throughout the year, every year.

THE HEAVIEST BURDEN FALLS, naturally, on the Queen herself. It is she who, as Head of State, is the focus for national life and government. Every year there are annual events at which the Queen must perform in an almost ritual manner. Her role as monarch reaches back far into history; the formalities of today are direct reminders of her ancestors' role as absolute sovereigns, and of the constraints placed upon them.

Facing page: the Queen waves to the crowd during her very successful state visit to Singapore in October, 1989. All members of the Royal Family undertake arduous foreign tours as part of their official duties. Left and below: the Queen attending the annual Maunday Thursday Ceremony at which she distributes gifts of specially minted silver coins to selected individuals. The custom was abandoned for some years during the seventeenth century, but was later revived to become one of the major royal ceremonies.

THE FIRST OF THE GREAT annual ceremonies is that of Royal Maundy, held on the Thursday before Easter. According to medieval theology the king was appointed by Christ to rule the nation and was expected to demonstrate certain Christ-like traits. Edward I introduced the Royal Maundy service to reflect Christ's washing of his disciples feet before the Last Supper. He washed and kissed the feet of poor subjects, and gave them gifts of clothing and food. The custom first changed under Elizabeth I who insisted that the dirty feet of the beggars be first cleaned by the Lord High Almoner. The foot-washing was abandoned altogether about a century later.

TODAY, THE QUEEN DISTRIBUTES Maundy Money in lieu of the provisions handed over by her predecessors. A total of £5.50 in normal currency is given. Much more highly prized is the specially minted Maundy Money which is distributed late in the

service. The coins are of sterling silver and in denominations of one penny, tuppence, threepence and a groat, a coin worth four pennies. These silver coins are minted at the same weight as the original silver penny of Edward I and are highly sought by coin collectors. Each recipient is given a purse containing as many pence as the monarch's age.

ONE OF THE MOST important roles of the medieval monarch was that of warrior. Kings were almost constantly in the saddle fighting off foreign invasion or dealing with internal rebellions and feuding. It was only success on the battlefield which ensured that a king, or queen, was able to maintain a secure hold on the crown and ensure peace in the kingdom. Some monarchs made such a success of fighting that they became famous as warriors.

KING RICHARD I IS perhaps the best-known of the Queen's warrior-king ancestors. In 1192 Richard was in the Holy Land and fighting at Jaffa. After leading a ferocious charge which cut down dozens of Moslems, King Richard rode alone to the enemy's ranks and challenged them to fight. So great was his reputation that none of them moved forward.

TODAY, THE QUEEN IS the official head of the armed services and they owe allegiance to her rather than to the government. Though in practice it is the government which makes wars and issues orders to generals, the theory that the Queen is Commander in Chief allows the nation to rally behind the national cause in times of war, whatever its feelings towards the politicians in control. It also has the useful effect of removing from any unscrupulous politician the possibility of using the military for the furtherance of his ambition. This role as a stabilising influence in changing times is one of the most important the Royal Family fulfils.

THE GREATEST ANNUAL AFFIRMATION of the Queen's military role is the Trooping the Colour ceremony held on the second Saturday in June. The Queen, escorted by the colonels of the guards and a troop of Household Cavalry, leaves Buckingham Palace to process along the Mall and arrive at Horse Guards Parade at 11 o'clock. Already on Horse Guards Parade are some 700 guardsmen, the massed bands and the Household Cavalry. For the following hour the troops march and process as they salute their monarch and colonel-in-chief.

THE HIGHLIGHT OF THE ceremony is the Trooping itself. This involves the colours presented to the regiment by the monarch being paraded through the ranks. The Trooping has its origins centuries ago when the regimental flag was marched through the ranks each morning in order to familiarise the soldiers with the banner. During the heat of battle soldiers were expected to rally around their regimental flag, so it was essential that they could recognise it. Having Trooped the Colour, the guards regiments march past the Queen before leaving the parade ground with the Queen and returning to barracks.

THE LAST BRITISH MONARCH to lead troops on the field of battle was King George II. In 1743 King George was campaigning on the Main River in Germany when he marched his army of 40,000 into a trap laid by a French force of 60,000. Once fighting began, however, the king led his troops well, blasting a gap in the French lines with steady musketry and a spirited cavalry charge. Thereafter monarchs were happy to leave the conduct of warfare in the hands of their generals.

The Queen drives to the 1990 Trooping the Colour ceremony in an open carriage after deciding to give up riding to the event.

THOUGH MONARCHS ARE NOW considered too valuable to risk their lives on the battlefield, the same is not true of other members of the Royal Family. A military career is considered almost essential to a royal prince, and most spend at least some time in the services. When war breaks out they take their place in the firing line, providing an example to others.

DURING THE FIRST WORLD WAR, Prince Albert, later King George VI, was a young lieutenant in the Royal Navy. In May, 1916, his ship received word that the German High Seas Fleet was at sea and, in company with the entire British Grand Fleet, she put to sea. During the ensuing Battle of Jutland, Prince Albert stuck firmly to his post in the forward gun turret of the cruiser HMS *Collingwood*. Even when the *Collingwood* was exchanging shell for shell with the German *Lutzow* at point-blank range, the young Prince did not flinch and was later commended in despatches. Such heroic action irritated his elder brother, the Prince of Wales and later Edward VIII. As heir to the throne he was forbidden to enter any combat zone.

DURING THE SECOND WORLD WAR the former combatant of Jutland was removed from the combat to fulfil his role as king. Nevertheless, King George shared the dangers of his subjects for Buckingham Palace was bombed more than once. It is rumoured that one unexploded bomb remains buried deep beneath the garden. In 1942 the King's younger brother, the Duke of Kent, was killed when his RAF aircraft smashed into a mountainside. His nephew, Patrick, Master of Glamis, was killed leading his Scottish regiment into battle in 1944.

THE MEMBER OF TODAY'S Royal Family who saw most active service during World War II was undoubtedly Prince Philip, now Duke of Edinburgh, though at the time he was only distantly related. Like his future father-in-law, Prince Philip served as a lieutenant in the Royal Navy. He saw action in the Mediterranean against the Italian Navy, risking his life under fire for his adopted country.

IN MORE RECENT YEARS it is Prince Andrew, who has most conspicuously continued the Royal fighting tradition. In 1982 Argentina invaded the Falkland Islands and Britain sent a task force south to recapture them. One of the premier ships to steam out of Portsmouth was HMS *Invincible*, an aircraft carrier on which served Prince Andrew. As a helicopter pilot Prince Andrew had many duties, including transporting

Below: Prince Charles wearing the red beret of the Parachute Regiment, of which he is the Colonel-in-Chief. Bottom: the Prince of Wales when in command of the minesweeper HMS *Bronnington* in 1975.

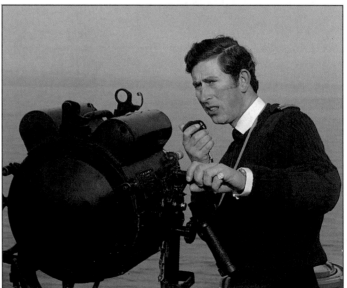

stores from ship to shore. But by far his most nerve-racking task was to hover his helicopter close to his parent ship in the hope of decoying a deadly Exocet missile from the more important target. As with his forbears, Prince Andrew acquitted himself well under fire and returned home to a rapturous welcome from his family.

PRINCE ANDREW'S RELATIVES HAVE also served their time in the services. The present Duke of Kent is Colonel of the Scots Guards and Prince Edward served for a time in the Royal Marines. But it is Prince Charles who has perhaps the most far-ranging military experience. As Prince of Wales he holds honorary rank in several military organisations and is Colonel of the Welsh Guards, but he has gained practical experience as well. In 1975 his lengthy service with the Royal Navy came to a climax when he was appointed commander of HMS *Bronnington*, a minesweeper. The following year he commanded his ship in an arduous naval exercise in the Firth of Forth. Soon afterwards his increasing duties as Prince of Wales forced Prince Charles to give up his full-time naval career.

IN NOVEMBER THE THIRD essential constitutional feature of the monarchy is emphasised, that of its relationship with Parliament. The State Opening of Parliament is rich with both the symbolism and the reality of power. At no other time are the history and modern face of the relationship between state and monarch so clearly shown.

BRITISH MONARCHS ONCE HELD absolute power, at least in theory. In practice their authority was always limited by the power of barons, nobles, the Church and other

Top: Prince Andrew beside his naval helicopter. Above: Lord Louis Mountbatten, who was killed by the IRA. He was a hero of Prince Charles.

elements of society. As early as the seventh century kings were recognising laws to which everyone, even themselves, were subject. Even the choice of king was subject to the nobles. It was the Witan, or council of great nobles, who chose the next king when one died. It was customary to select a member of the Royal Family, but this rule was sometimes broken.

AS TIME PASSED THE Crown found itself increasingly hedged in by constraints. The Magna Carta, signed by King John in 1215, is the most famous of several concessions made by British monarchs to their subjects. As first the nobles and later the town guilds and merchants increased their prosperity and influence the Crown saw its power weaken. In theory, however, the power of the monarch was undiminished. Forceful and able sovereigns, such as Henry VIII or Elizabeth I, could juggle prestige, patronage and authority to keep the forces within society in check and maintain the impression of regal control.

BY THE MID-SEVENTEENTH CENTURY the struggle between the Crown and the citizens for real political power became increasingly open. King Charles I attempted to regain the reality of royal authority under the outdated concept of the Divine Right of Kings, which asserted that God had given him the nation to rule. Neither the nobles nor the commoners were happy to submit to such autocracy. The legal struggle between King and Parliament continued for some years until, in 1642, the King raised the Royal Standard and the Civil War began.

PARLIAMENT EMERGED SUCCESSFUL FROM the struggle, executed the King in 1649 and abolished the monarchy. The experiment with a Republic lasted just eleven years. In 1658 Oliver Cromwell, who had become Protector with almost dictatorial powers, died and power fell into the hands of the generals. Two years later the most powerful general, George Monk, Duke of Albemarle, recalled Charles II from exile and placed him on the throne. Though the new King sat on his throne, Parliament retained many powers won during the Civil War.

Above, above left and top: the Queen drives to Westminster for the State Opening of Parliament, accompanied by a ceremonial troop of the Life Guards. This regiment was raised in 1660 from the Cavaliers and noblemen who had accompanied King Charles II into exile after the Civil War. Until 1788 the regiment remained firmly closed to all but the social elite.

TODAY, THE AUTHORITY TO govern resides in the House of Commons and with the democratically elected government. That authority is, in theory, derived from permission from the Crown and all actions are carried out in the name of Her Majesty. The monarch remains the Head of State and is able to override Parliament in emergencies. No monarch has attempted such a drastic step for nearly three centuries.

THE STATE OPENING OF PARLIAMENT plays out the shifting basis of power through symbolism and ceremony which last for much of the day and involve the most glittering and impressive royal show staged annually.

THE DAY'S CEREMONIAL OPENS when some of the crown jewels leave the Tower of London. The Imperial State Crown and the Cap of Maintenance, together with other regalia, are removed from the strong-room at the Tower and placed in a state coach by the Comptroller of the Lord Chamberlain's Office. The coach then

Below: the royal procession moves through the Palace of Westminster on its way to the House of Lords. In medieval times Parliament was summoned by the monarch when he wished to consult the people about a difficult problem or to raise money. It was usually dissolved after only a few days.

processes through the streets to the Palace of Westminster, escorted by a corporal and six troopers from the Household Cavalry. The symbols of regal power are carried into the sovereign's robing room ready for use.

MEANWHILE, THE QUEEN LEAVES Buckingham Palace in another state coach accompanied by the Duke of Edinburgh and the Prince of Wales. On arriving at the Palace of Westminster the Queen receives a royal salute from the guard of honour formed from the Household Cavalry. The Royal Standard, the flag of the monarch, is raised over the Palace to signify that the sovereign is in residence.

HAVING BEEN ROBED AND crowned, the Queen marches in procession through the Palace to the House of Lords. Here is seen all the panoply of medieval symbolism which once echoed the real power held by the monarch.

THE CROWN ITSELF IS a highly jewelled example of the ceremonial hat won by those in power for centuries. The oldest crowns still in existence are the iron crown of Lombardy and Charlemagne's crown, both over a thousand years old. The original crown of England was a relatively unimposing circlet of gold. It was melted down by Oliver Cromwell, but some of the metal was saved and incorporated in St Edward's Crown, which is used at coronations. Dukes and other nobles are permitted to wear coronets, but only the reigning monarch, and his queen if he is a king, can wear a crown.

THE SWORD OF STATE IS carried before the Queen in the procession. This magnificently jewelled weapon is based on the large, medieval, double-handed sword which was wielded in battle by only the strongest of fighters. This symbolises the power of the state and, in medieval days, could only be used by the king. Swords were both expensive and highly prized. Most knights guarded their swords jealously and might pass them on to their sons. Particularly keen-edged swords were given names such as 'Brain-biter' or 'Blood-lover' and became as famous as their owners. Excalibur, which is said to have been used by King Arthur, is one sword to have achieved mythical status.

DURING THE PROCESSION THROUGH the Palace of Westminster to the House of Lords, the Queen is accompanied by the Officers of State. The two most important of these are the Lord Great Chamberlain and the Earl Marshal, offices which once controlled great power but are now merely ceremonial. Both posts were originally those for servants close to the monarch. As time passed the monarch used these close servants for increasingly important duties, until by the late middle ages their positions were reserved for the highest nobility.

THE CHAMBERLAIN ORIGINALLY ATTENDED to the king's household, controlling royal expenditure. Today, he is responsible for organising those ceremonies which take place indoors. The Earl Marshal was once the supreme commander of the king's army, but is now restricted to organising processions and outdoor ceremonies. These two officers are accompanied by others, such as the Kings of Arms, responsible for heraldry; the Lord High Chancellor, who keeps the Great Seal; and the Lord Privy Seal.

ENTERING THE HOUSE OF LORDS, the Queen seats herself on the magnificent royal throne of state, flanked by the Duke of Edinburgh and the Prince of Wales. Here, dressed in her robes and crown and surrounded by the nobles, she exhibits all the panoply of royal power.

AT THIS POINT THE Queen's official messenger, Black Rod, departs to summon the House of Commons to the House of Lords. As he approaches the Commons, the door is slammed in his face, showing the power of the Commons to exclude who they wish. After knocking, Black Rod enters and invites the Commons to the Lords. Processing in an informal bunch and chatting amongst themselves, the Commons contrast strongly with the dignified behaviour of the House of Lords. Once the Commons are in the Lords' chamber the Queen can officially open Parliament and make her speech.

IT IS AT THIS POINT that the show of regal power is replaced by the reality of democracy. The speech made by the Queen outlines the legislation which her ministers will introduce to Parliament. The speech is written by the ministers and they alone decide what legislation they shall formulate. The Queen has no say whatever in the speech she must deliver.

BUT THE QUEEN'S ROLE in government is not restricted to a single ceremony. She receives a weekly visit from the Prime Minister and has the right to be consulted on any proposed legislation. Having been involved in affairs of state at the highest level for nearly thirty years, the Queen has a wealth of experience and wisdom

Facing page: the Queen and Prince Phillip seated on the gilded and gem-encrusted thrones of the House of Lords for the State Opening of Parliament. In former days the monarch would listen to Parliament and then decide what action the country should take, but today Parliament alone decides how to govern the nation.

Above: the silver-topped baton of one of the drum majors of the Guards. These band leaders have richly decorated uniforms and use the baton to conduct the musicians marching behind them.

which she can make available to any government, particularly one under a new Prime Minister. Though she has little actual power, the Queen is able to influence ministers to a large degree.

ALL THE DUTIES AND responsibilities of the Royal Family, and they are many, are dependent upon the central position of the monarch within the constitution and society of Britain. Without these responsibilities, the rest of the Royal Family would have only a small role to play in Britain.

IN 1969 PRINCE CHARLES was invested as Prince of Wales at Caernarvon Castle and presented to the people of the Principality. Since that time he has tirelessly carried out his duties as Prince of Wales and Duke of Cornwall. The latter is very much a working appointment. The Duchy owns vast estates throughout the country and is responsible for both urban developments and rural conservation. As Duke, Prince Charles has established a fine reputation as a diligent landlord. He has worked to improve his lands and properties, while at the same time remaining firmly committed to conservation. Each year the Prince spends some time on an ordinary farm on his estates.

AS PRINCE OF WALES, Prince Charles duties have been far more public. It is in this role that the Prince is called upon to help various worthy causes and to attend numerous functions. Among other organisations, Prince Charles is patron of the Prince's Trust, Business in the Community and the Prince of Wales Awards for Industrial Innovation. All of his numerous connections take up a great deal of his time, which must be rationed firmly.

SINCE 1981 PRINCE CHARLES has had a companion to help him with his official tasks. On 29th July in that year he married Lady Diana Spencer in one of the most glittering royal occasions of the century. Before the announcement of the engagement press speculation had been high that Lady Diana and Prince Charles might become married so the formal declaration raised few eyebrows.

FROM THE MOMENT SHE entered the public eye, the Princess of Wales has been a great success. For her official engagement photo call the future Princess wore a navy blue suit with a drawstring waisted jacket and a bowed blouse. The wedding dress, which created a great stir, was created by top fashion designers, the Emmanuels. As suited a fairy-tale wedding, the dress was rich with frills, puff sleeves and yards of silk.

SINCE THEN DIANA HAS established herself as a major trend-setter within the fashion world. Rarely has her innate good taste deserted her. One of her most notable fashion mistakes would scarcely have been remarked upon on anyone else. At a ballet performance attended as part of an official visit to Portugal in February, 1987, the Princess arrived wearing a fine black taffeta dress with a choker in the form of a black bow-tie. Over this was an orange jacket of glittering satin. Somehow the bright jacket struck a comical air with the shirtless bow-tie. Apart from such minor set backs, though, the Princess of Wales has turned in an almost faultless performance.

THE FASHION WORLD HAS revelled in dressing the Princess of Wales. She has the type of figure in which designers delight. Since she is very tall and slim, the Princess has the stature to carry off outfits which would be quite unsuitable on shorter, stouter figures.

ONE OF THE MOST innovative of these ensembles was seen at the opening of the Hong Kong Cultural Centre in Kowloon during a tour of the Far East in November, 1989. The outfit consisted of a full-length white evening gown embroidered with beads,

From the day of her wedding, and even before, the Princess of Wales has been recognised as a leader of fashion. Her wedding dress was highly acclaimed and since then her lead in taste has been followed by many fashion houses.

especially around the neckline, which was stiff with beads. Over this was worn an open, waist-length jacket with elbow-length sleeves and a stiff collar which stood up like that of an eighteenth-century fop. The glittering outfit was topped off by the diamond-and-pearl tiara which the Princess was given as a wedding present by the Queen.

SUCH FORMAL OCCASIONS HAVE become a regular feature in Diana's life since her marriage. In the course of the same Far Eastern tour she also visited the Indonesian cultural park of Taman Mini and watched a display of traditional dancing at the Karaton Palace at the invitation of the Sultan of Yogyakarta. Less formally, the Princess of Wales visited the Sitanala Leprosy Hospital where sufferers of this dread disease are treated.

MORE RECENTLY THE PRINCE and Princess of Wales have undertaken an official visit to Hungary. The visit needed handling with some delicacy. Less than a month earlier the East European nation had held its first democratic elections for forty years, after the Communist government had been forced to concede democracy. The tour was widely seen as a British seal of approval on the Hungarians' move towards democracy.

ON THE EVENING OF their arrival the Prince and Princess of Wales were entertained by the newly elected Parliament to a sumptuous state dinner. The Princess chose to wear the stunning beaded white evening gown last seen in Hong Kong. This time she discarded the startling jacket and instead wore a seven-strand pearl choker. The next day the Royal couple visited the University of Economic Sciences where Prince Charles gave a surprisingly frank speech on what he saw as the virtues of democracy and the iniquities of Communism. The Princess later visited the Peto Institute where children suffering from cerebral palsy are treated. The Princess' love of children is well known and this visit only served to emphasise that fondness.

THE PRINCE AND PRINCESS, of course, have two children of their own, Prince Harry and Prince William. Prince William made an early debut on the royal scene in March, 1983, at the age of just nine months. The Prince and Princess of Wales were due to undertake a lengthy tour of Australia and New Zealand. It was widely reported that the Princess refused to be parted from her new baby and so Prince William broke royal tradition by accompanying his parents on a formal tour. He did not, however, take much part in the various duties of the trip. After being displayed to the cameras on arrival at Alice Springs Airport, Prince William remained with his nanny while the Prince and Princess of Wales attended events.

BOTH PRINCE WILLIAM AND his younger brother attend Wetherby School in Notting Hill. It is not at all an unusual sight for photographers to see the Princess of Wales dropping the boys off at the school. On one memorable occasion in 1989 the Princess arrived wearing a baggy sweatshirt, equally baggy trousers, a man's jacket and cowboy boots. The event sparked discussion on a BBC chat show as to whether or not mothers should dress fashionably when taking children to school. It was felt that such display might embarrass the child.

IN CONTRAST, THE QUEEN Mother always believes in dressing well. In 1940 she was due to visit bomb victims in London's East End when a well-meaning courtier suggested she should wear more suitable clothing. 'I always wear my best clothes when visiting friends' replied the then Queen Elizabeth.

INDEED, SINCE SHE FIRST came into the royal limelight in the 1920s, when she married the future King George VI, the Queen Mother has become famous for her unremitting

Facing page: the two sons of the Prince and Princess of Wales, Prince Harry (on the left) and Prince William. At his mother's insistence, Prince William (remaining pictures) accompanied his parents on an official visit to Australia when he was just nine months old.

charm and distinctive dress sense. The wedding of 26th April, 1923, was notable for the wedding gown which was the height of period fashion and for the matching gowns of the eight bridesmaids. The unexpected abdication of King Edward VIII propelled the then Duchess of York onto the throne as Queen of George VI after a bitter national debate and only three years before the outbreak of the Second World War.

TODAY, THE QUEEN MOTHER is often hailed as the nation's grandmother. She has certainly established a much-loved role for herself during her daughter's reign. Now in her nineties, the Queen Mother still undertakes a number of official engagements for favourite organisations, such as the Royal Hospital and Home, or the Friends of St Paul's Cathedral.

Ever since she first entered the royal scene in 1923 as the Duchess of York, Queen Elizabeth, the Queen Mother, has been a great favourite with the crowds. Her cheerful, ready smile and unfailing good manners have ensured that her visits are eagerly sought after by numerous organisations. Today the Queen Mother undertakes fewer engagements than she once did, but her schedule is still surprisingly busy for a lady of such an advanced age. There is no doubt that she carries her years extremely well.

INEVITABLY THE QUEEN MOTHER undertakes fewer official engagements now than formerly and her place is being taken by the younger royals. Perhaps the most indefatigable of these is the Princess Royal, who has become known and highly respected for her arduous tours and programmes on behalf of various organisations.

PRINCESS ANNE'S ASSOCIATION WITH the Save the Children Fund has taken her to many parts of the world, including some rather hazardous places. She has flown into war regions to visit volunteers working with refugees and children in desperate need. Local governments and guerilla leaders are not always appreciative of such visits and suspicion often lurks near the surface. An advance party of people responsible for organising Princess Anne's visit were held at gunpoint while their credentials were examined in one African nation.

MUCH OF PRINCESS ANNE'S work is carried out away from the direct limelight attracted by other members of her family. But in June, 1990, she toured the Soviet Union for thirteen days, becoming the first member of the Royal Family to visit the Soviet

Union since the Communists murdered their own royal family in 1918. The visit marked perhaps the high point of international recognition of reforms introduced by President Gorbachev.

ALSO SOMEWHAT OUT OF the public eye are the Duke and Duchess of York. The Duke's full-time military career does not permit him the time necessary to undertake a full public programme, but the Duchess does much to make up for that. Among other organisations she is patron of the Leukaemia Research Fund, the Motor Neurone Disease Association and the Samaritans, all of which keep her busy with numerous functions.

Above: the Duke and Duchess of York with their first child, Princess Beatrice. Facing page top: the ever gracious Princess Michael of Kent. Facing page bottom: the Duchess of Kent speaks to an overwhelmed child on a walkabout.

IN FEBRUARY, 1990, THE Duchess travelled to the French Alps to present awards for the Combined Services Skiing Championships, despite the fact that she was expecting her second child shortly. On 23rd March the baby duly arrived at the Portland Hospital. The Duke was on naval duty at the time and arrived at the hospital with little time to spare. A week after the birth the Duchess left the hospital looking extremely well in a pink and white satin outfit. The daughter was later named Eugenie Victoria Helena, following the Yorks' preference for old names. Their first daughter is named Beatrice.

THE BIRTH OF THE new princess did not hold her mother back from her round of official engagements. In June she was even called upon to inspect sheep and cattle at the West Sussex Annual Show. In company with her husband, the Duchess later attended a dedication service in York Minster, being patron of the York Minster Trust, but she attended the Trooping the Colour alone. Along with many naval wives she spends long periods of time apart from her husband. During the Gulf Crisis the Duchess spent time with other service wives while their husbands were away facing the enemy.

THOUGH THE DUCHESS IS not so widely favoured by the fashion world as the perfect model for their designs, nonetheless she has a distinctive style which has attracted its followers. Her wedding gown was widely acclaimed at the time, being a vision of silk with pearl and sequin embroidery and a seventeen-foot-long train. Even before the wedding, the future Duchess had begun to contribute to the fashion scene with her famous bows, which appeared in all sorts of positions. Since her wedding the Duchess has favoured designers such as Roberto Devorik, Lindka Ceirach and Gina Fratini. Together they have produced a series of stunning outfits for the Duchess' use at official and unofficial engagements.

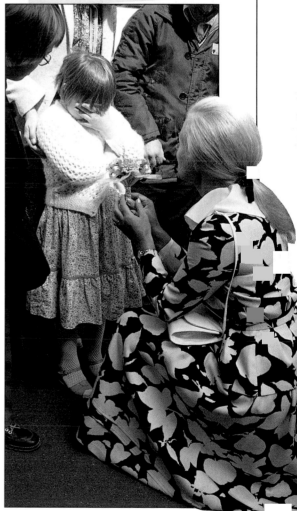

EVEN THOSE MEMBERS OF the Royal Family not immediately related to the Queen are expected to fulfil public roles. The constitutional role of the monarch can reach across the generations to involve cousins and uncles as well as brothers and children.

THE DUKE AND DUCHESS of Kent are perhaps best known for their patronage of the Wimbledon Tennis Championships, at which they present the prizes each year. The couple are, however, frequently called upon to perform visits and carry out engagements. The Duchess, in particular, has been widely regarded for her effortless tact and charm. Prince and Princess Michael of Kent carry out a number of functions; the Prince is known to be fascinated by vintage motor cars, while the Princess is the Patron of the Arab Horse Society. The Gloucesters too are called upon to lend their time and patronage to a number of causes.

CENTRAL TO THE ROYAL FAMILY'S role within the nation is the position of the monarch as Head of State. It is this which accounts for the great annual ceremonials which mark the state calendar. But the duties and responsibilities of the Royal Family go much further and embrace a great range of charitable and admirable events. The Royal Family has not been found wanting in its dedication to the nation and its people.

Left: the Princess of Wales accompanies her sons, Prince William and Prince Henry, in a chair lift at the skiing resort of Klosters, where she and her husband annually take a holiday. The Princess (below) is a competent skier and no doubt this early introduction to the sport means that her children will be too.

It is known that both the Prince and the Princess of Wales prefer not to have to pose for photographs during what is meant to be a private holiday, so a photo session is arranged at the beginning of their time at Klosters when journalists are given an opportunity to take all the shots they need. Afterwards, the Prince and Princess are free to enjoy their winter break undisturbed.

The British weather is no kinder to the Royal Family than to the rest of us. They too have to battle against wind and cold (below, bottom and facing page). Right: Princess Anne wrapped up against the rain.

It is an essential part of the official duties of every member of the Royal Family to meet the people in a wide variety of circumstances. From her earliest contact with the public during her short engagement, the Princess of Wales has been particularly adept at this skill, especially where children are involved. On walkabouts during official visits, the Princess often makes time for children in the crowd and many believe she looks at her happiest when in the company of youngsters. Above: the Prince and Princess of Wales in a crowd of children during their tour of Australia in 1983.

The Queen's fondness for corgis is well known – she took one on her honeymoon – and they always accompany her on her holidays in the country. Other members of the Royal Family keep a variety of dogs both as pets and as working animals.

OAK APPLE DAY

On Oak Apple Day veteran soldiers at the Royal Hospital, Chelsea, celebrate the birthday of the hospital's founder, King Charles II. The Chelsea Pensioners, dressed in light scarlet uniforms, parade in the central quadrangle carrying sprigs of oak. On this day oak foliage surrounds the large bronze of Charles II in the grounds, in front of which the Sovereign stands during the parade.

O BELLOQUE FRACTORUM CONDIDIT CAROLUS SECUNDUS

Princess Diana is known to have a penchant for dramatic, off-the-shoulder evening gowns (right), but rarely has she worn a dress more typical of a fairytale princess than her glorious sequin and chiffon creation (below). Remaining pictures: sashes and ties, a feature of Diana's day outfits.

Exotic locations are encountered by
the Queen on her wide-ranging state
visits to various parts of the world.
When touring the South Sea Islands,
she and Prince Philip were shown
fascinating displays of local colour.
They were paddled ashore at Tuvalu
(top left) and encountered warriors
in war paint (top), as well as an
absorbing array of ceremonial
regalia (left and facing page).

The Queen Mother's birthday on 4th August has become a regular occasion in the unofficial royal calendar of events. Each year a crowd of well-wishers gathers outside Clarence House in London to help her celebrate. Without fail the Queen Mother appears to acknowledge the crowd, with as many members of her family as are present. After gathering gifts and cards, she retires to her home for more intimate celebrations. Above: Princess Diana and the Queen Mother at Royal Ascot.

The Queen is recognised as being a foremost authority on bloodstock breeding. Facing page: Her Majesty absorbed by an equestrian event.

These pages: Prince William and Prince Henry, the sons of the Prince and Princess of Wales, in their early years. Royal children are of endless fascination to the public and photographs of the toddlers receive a ready welcome. Photos such as these are eagerly sought after.

The young princes have quite different characters: Prince Harry is quieter than Prince William. Both, though, are clearly their parents' pride and joy.

Wherever the Royal Family appears in public they receive a rapturous welcome and there are always those eager to present small gifts of flowers or similar trinkets. The Princess of Wales is able to make everyone feel that their own contribution to a big day is somehow special, which is one of the reasons for her continuing popularity with the public.

Prince Charles is a well-known and adventurous horseman. He has ridden in steeplechases and taken part in hunts and cross-country rides. However his favourite equestrian sport appears to be polo. A serious injury in 1990, when he fractured his arm in two places, has failed to put him off the sport and he continues to play, often watched by members of his family (right).

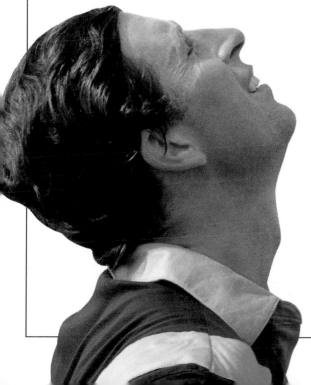

The wedding of the Prince of Wales to Lady Diana Spencer was watched by hundreds of thousands who packed the streets of London and by millions more who watched the events unfold on television around the world.

Headgear for the Queen ranges from the glamorous and formal tiara for evening occasions to the starkly functional scarf. Custom dictates that whatever the Queen wears, it should not obstruct either her view, or prevent the public from seeing her face.

The presence of visiting royalty often encourages local people to excel themselves in their choice of attire. Some dress in their finest clothes, while others don traditional costumes of great colour and display. The travels of the members of the Royal Family bring them into contact with a vast range of eccentrically dressed individuals all over the world.

Riding to hounds has been a favourite equestrian sport of the rural aristocracy since the eighteenth century, when the hunting of foxes changed from a purely functional exercise to an elaborate social occasion. Prince Charles rides to hounds, following the lead of his predecessor as Prince of Wales, the Prince Regent, later King George IV, who had a considerable reputation as an enthusiastic and able sportsman.

Facing page: Princess Beatrice, (right) Prince Henry, (below) Peter Phillips and (bottom) Zara Phillips. The royal cousins' development is followed avidly by the public, an interest which is not new. The future George VI once said "My chief claim to fame seems to be that I am the father of Princess Elizabeth."

The Queen's official birthday is in
June, a month chosen so that there
was the best chance of fine weather
for the outdoor ceremonials. But
June is not always sunny, and the
Trooping the Colour is carried out
whatever the weather. When the
rains come all that the Queen, her
entourage and the Guards on parade
can do is grin and bear it.

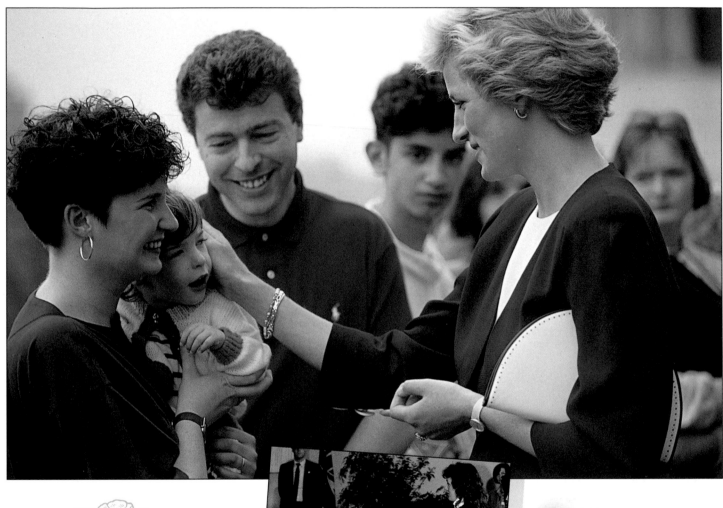

Two royal ladies who demonstrate especial charm and natural ease in their dealings with members of the public are the Princess of Wales (above and right) and the Duchess of Kent (far right and facing page). Neither was brought up to be a member of the Royal Family – both married into it and learnt their new role by practice and hard work, rather than by long years of instruction at the hands of courtiers.

When 'on duty' at official functions
the members of the Royal Family
take great care in choosing their
dress. When relaxing in private,
however, royalty is inclined to be
rather more casual and some
charmingly informal outfits may
be spotted.

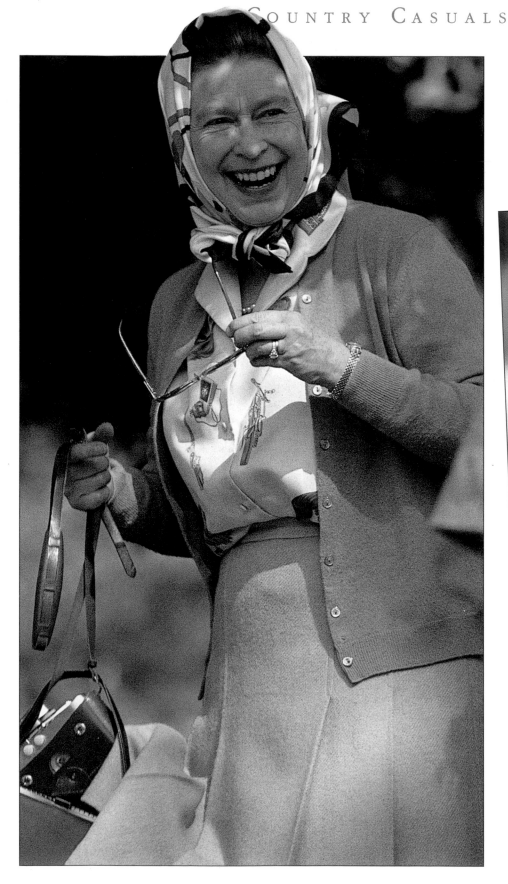

Equestrian events see the Queen
(left) in her headscarf, Princess
Diana in a casual sweatshirt (above)
and Princess Anne's children, Peter
and Zara (facing page), in jeans.

The annual Trooping the Colour ceremony is attended by men of the various Guards regiments. The oldest of these is the Coldstream Guards, raised in 1650, and the youngest the Welsh Guards of 1915.

The Princess of Wales is known as a setter of fashion, not only for her consistent good taste but also because she has a tall, slim, model-type figure which shows off most ensembles very well.

Before Princess Diana's marriage, when she was Lady Diana Spencer, she once acted as photographic model for a distinguished designer. Since her marriage the Princess has worn clothing by an exciting range of designers and has been snapped by photographers in a wide variety of outfits. It is extremely rare to see her wearing something that does not suit her.

The Queen's historic visit to China brought her and Prince Philip into close contact with both the Communist present of the country and its Imperial past. Spectacular pageants were staged as a welcome by the authorities, marshalling hundreds of individuals and elaborately designed dragon dancers in unison (above, right and facing page top left).

The Great Wall of China (right), begun around 200 BC to keep out savage northern barbarians, and the terracotta army (bottom), buried soon afterwards to guard a deceased emperor, were both visited by the Queen and Prince Philip on their Chinese tour.

In 1982 Prince Andrew sailed to the Falkland Islands as a helicopter pilot aboard HMS *Invincible* to form part of the British task force sent to recapture the islands from the Argentinians. After a successful campaign, with no little danger to himself, Prince Andrew returned to be greeted by his mother and other members of the Royal Family at Portsmouth.

The new generation of the Royal Family is being brought up to appreciate equestrian sports. Left: Prince Charles leads his sons in Windsor Great Park and (below) Princess Anne introduces a young Peter Phillips to a team of Shires. Bottom: (left) Princess Michael of Kent, a keen rider, and (right) Peter Phillips ready to follow the horses.

Facing page: the Duchess of York leaves the Portland Hospital with her second daughter, Princess Eugenie, on 30th March, 1990. Her elder daughter, Princess Beatrice (above), was born two years earlier and is already learning to ski.

Royal children are usually kept out of the glare of publicity, but the Prince and Princess of Wales are aware that Prince William will have an increasingly public role to play, and so involve him in a number of official engagements. His first ever was at Cardiff (left) in March, 1991.

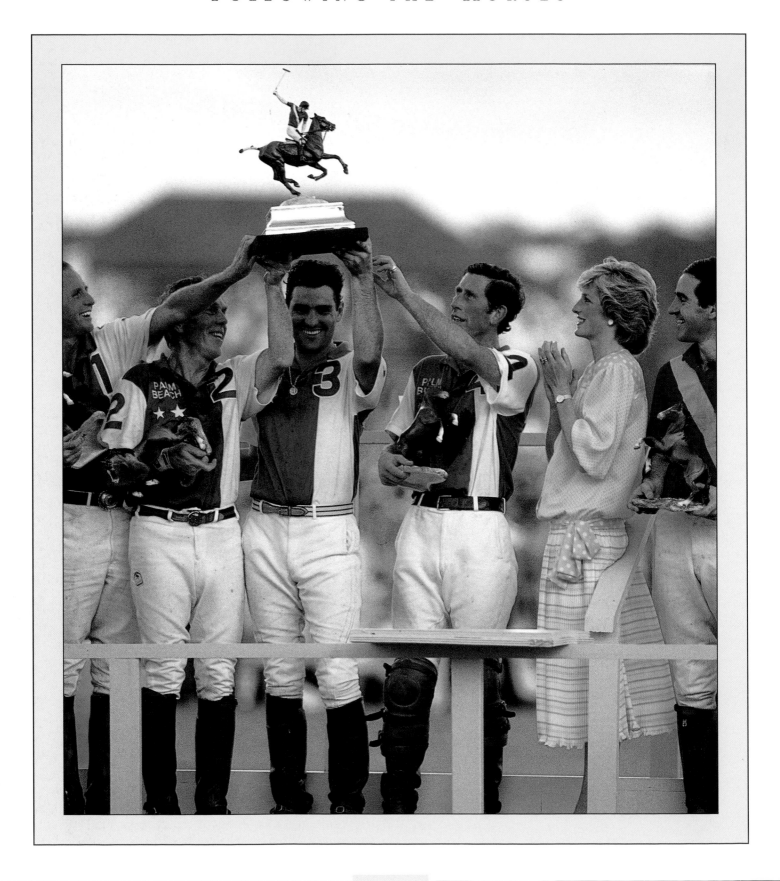

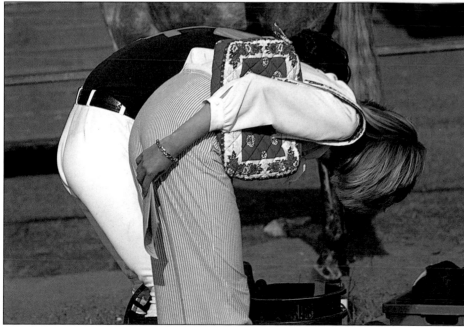

Prince Charles is committed to polo and has enjoyed considerable success with this sport. Other members of the family are often in attendance at his games.

The annual Garter Service, held at St George's Chapel in Windsor Castle, brings together the premier knights of England. Each Knight of the Garter has his or her own stall above which hangs their banner and helmet. When the knight dies a plaque carrying his coat of arms is fixed to the back of the stall.

The Order of the Garter dates back to 1344 when King Edward III instituted the order to include the noblest knights in Christendom. Later Edward added the Military Knights to the order. The king was said to be inspired by the legendary Knights of the Round Table.

That Princess Diana has good fashion taste is well known, but her other interests are not always so well publicised. Among other things the Princess of Wales is reported to be fond of music by composers as diverse as Tchaikovsky and David Bowie, to read novels by Jeffrey Archer and to follow the Peanuts cartoon strip.

Guns occupy a smaller place in royal life than they did a generation or two ago when George V could lead a shoot which bagged 4,000 pheasants in one day. Right: Lord Lichfield at a clay pigeon shoot, a sport which remains popular, as do displays of marksmanship, (left) the Duke and Duchess of York in Canada and (below) the Queen in Africa.

Whenever the Queen pays an official visit she attracts ceremonial and protocol. Above: a ceremonial sunshade held over the Queen's head and (above right) an elaborate banquet, both in the Far East. Right: a ceremonial salute in Hyde Park from the King's Troop, Royal Horse Artillery on the occasion of the Queen's birthday on 21st April.

Right: a high security motor convoy. Below: the classic red carpet is unfurled in readiness for Her Majesty. Bottom: a formal night out at the opera.

Prince Philip, like most members of the Royal Family, is a keen horseman. His particular interest is four-in-hand driving, so named because four horses are driven independently by a single coach driver. Taking to the sport after giving up polo, the Prince competes in many events and has enjoyed some success in his chosen pursuit.

The Queen Mother is well known for her liking for pastel shades and for flowing gowns from a variety of designers which suit her mature years. The official Royal Warrant for her coats is held by Aquascutum.

Both the Duchess of York and the Princess of Wales are noted skiers, the Duchess being a Black Run skier. Both families favour the expensive Swiss resort of Klosters in the Alps for their skiing as it is sufficiently exclusive to ensure a modicum of privacy and offers challenging slopes and pistes to satisfy even the most adventurous sportsman. It is said, though, that the Princess' enthusiasm waned after the 1988 tragedy in which Major Hugh Lindsey died.

The wedding of the Duke and Duchess of York was held in Westminster Abbey on 23rd July 1986, the ninth royal wedding the Abbey has seen this century.

Since their wedding in 1947, the Queen and Prince Philip have made a formidable team. Taking on the undoubtedly difficult role of consort to the monarch, Prince Philip has made it particularly his own and works tirelessly. While unfailingly supporting his wife, Prince Philip has still managed to stamp his own strong character on the public consciousness.

Quiet moments of relaxation away from formal duties and the ever-present and inquisitive public are rare for members of the Royal Family and are to be enjoyed all the more for that. Facing page left: Prince Andrew and Princess Beatrice at the 1990 Windsor Horse Show when Prince Andrew was on leave.

Facing page top right: Prince Charles on the polo field. Facing page bottom right and right: Princess Diana, as elegant in casual wear as in formal clothes. Above: the Queen enjoying herself at a polo match.

As a young princess, the Queen enjoyed the fashion spotlight. This premier place may now be occupied by younger royal women, but the Queen's taste remains an important influence in the fashion world.

During a visit to India the Queen was brought face to face with the stark contrasts of that enormous land. The glittering wealth of the princes and the panoply of government were spread out for the state occasions (right, bottom and bottom right) of the visit. But the Queen was not content simply to indulge in the fabled wealth of India, she also visited Mother Teresa (below) to see for herself the dreadful poverty of the big city slums.

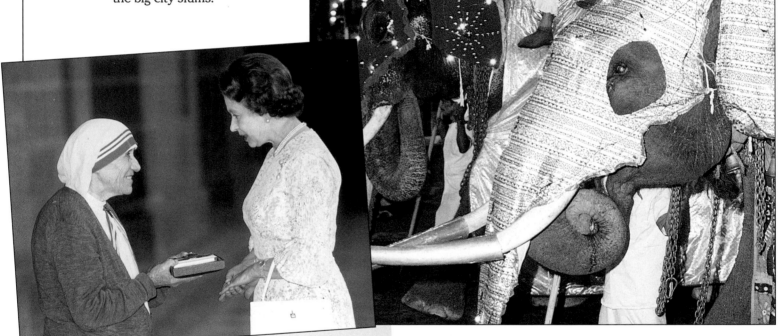

The Queen also found time during her visit to India to meet some of the saffron-robed Buddhist monks (right) of the Subcontinent, the numbers of which have been boosted by refugees from Tibet who were driven out of their country, along with their leader the Dalai Lama, by the Chinese authorities. Umbrellas were used to protect both monks and monarch from the sun.

Riders all. Facing page: Zara Phillips, (top) the Queen with President Reagan and (above) Prince Edward. Left: Princess Anne in competition and (far left) Prince Charles at polo.

A large part of the Royal Family's time is taken up with functions that duty demands they attend. An annual event that as many members as possible are present for is the Trooping the Colour ceremony, after which the family appear on the Buckingham Palace balcony (right).

Above: the Prince and Princess of Wales pass a member of the Swiss Guard before their audience with the Pope in the Vatican. The Princess is dressed in black, as is the custom for women on such occasions

Whatever the weather on the day, royal functions must go ahead as they have usually been arranged months in advance and any delay would disrupt the schedule of the following events. Fortunately, the royal entourage carries a wide range of weather-proof equipment.

These pages: the Princess of Wales with her children, Prince William and Prince Harry, enjoying a relaxing break on the ski slopes of Switzerland. The exclusive resort of Klosters is a favourite with the younger members of the Royal Family, but it was here that Prince Charles was almost killed when his skiing party was struck by an avalanche. A good friend of his, Major Hugh Lindsay, was swept away by the mass of snow and ice and his death highlighted the dangers of skiing off piste.

Princess Anne is a highly accomplished horsewoman and has competed in numerous events, even representing Great Britain in the Olympic Games. The most spectacular of the equestrian events she favours is the Three Day Event, which includes a demanding cross-country route over hazards that tax both horse and rider.

Princess Diana turns heads wherever she goes in the world, her innate dress sense ensuring that she inevitably looks the part, on land or on board ship.

The Princess of Wales has never been shy about trying bold new fashions and colour combinations. Her breathtaking black and white evening gown (above) is only one of many which have taken fellow dancers by surprise.

Facing page: Princess Michael of Kent. Below: cabinetmaker Viscount Linley, Princess Margaret's son. Bottom left: minding the children on the balcony after the Trooping the Colour. Bottom right: the Duke of Kent. Right: Princess Diana with Princess Margaret's daughter, Lady Sarah Armstrong-Jones.

Many members of the Royal Family spend more time meeting people than doing anything else. Not only are they formally introduced to local dignitaries on their numerous trips, but they also move among the crowds, stopping to chat informally to many of the ordinary people who have turned out to see them, some of whom will have waited for hours for the pleasure.

Polo is thought to be the fastest team game in the world. Prince Charles's passion for the sport is well known. Absorbed in a match, the Prince has few qualms about changing a shirt between chukas in full view of the public.

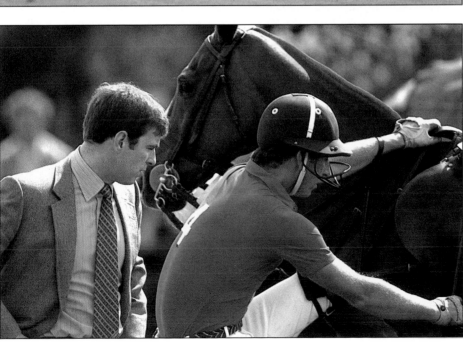

Left: Lady Sarah Armstrong-Jones, and (bottom) her mother, Princess Margaret. Below: the Duchess of Gloucester, who is deeply involved with musical events, being a talented amateur musician herself.

Above: Princess Alice, dowager Duchess of Gloucester, with her grandchildren. The Duchess led a highly active life, fulfilling many duties of a member of the Royal Family for decades, but in 1983 announced her retirement, though she maintained links with some of her favourite causes. Right: Prince and Princess Michael of Kent, who are not given any official duties, but who nonetheless attend about 100 functions each year.